Z-ANGELS

A gentle but powerful nudge in life comes
at the most opportune moment.
This is yours.

Jan Mayfield

Jan Mayfield

Copyright © by Jan Mayfield

Z-Angels A gentle but powerful nudge in life comes at the most opportune moment. This is yours.

Copyright notice

All rights reserved. No part of this publication may be reproduced, stored in a retrieval system or transmitted, in any form or by any means, without prior written permission of the publisher or author, nor be otherwise circulated in any form of binding or cover other than that in which it is published and without a similar condition being imposed on the subsequent purchaser.

The information in this book should not be treated as a substitute for professional medical advice.

All use of the information given in this book is at the reader's discretion.

The author or publisher is not responsible for your interpretations.

All quotes except where stated are the work of the author Jan Mayfield.

ISBN:978-1-8383132-4-1

Year published 2022

"My mother, I dedicate this book to you with blessings from your husband, my father, who supported us before his passing and now continues to guide and bring confirmations to us from his eternal home."

The power of love with the faith of above.

Dressed in diamonds glistening in God's light.

To ascend space and time.

Made in the universal grandeur of love and transmutation.

Snake in the passage of your divine time.

Grow in the love of the Z-Angels' light.

Blessed are those who travel this path.

You are here to project love to the world.

Contents

Preface	vii
CHAPTER 1	1
Introduction	1
Everything Begins to Make Sense	1
CHAPTER 2	9
This is New	9
Trusting in All I Do	9
CHAPTER 3	13
My Preparation	13
Hindsight is a Wonderful Thing	13
CHAPTER 4	29
God's Words	29
I Have To Do as I am Told	29
CHAPTER 5	33
This is New	33
Trusting in All I Do	33
CHAPTER 6	37
Delivery	37
Here are the Z-Angels	37
CHAPTER 7	41
Let's become Acquainted with the Four Angels	41
CHAPTER 8	47
Are You Ready?	47

The Time is Right for You to Meet Your True Self; the Z-Angels are Here to Give You that Opportunity ... 47

CHAPTER 9 ... 51
Sensing the Z-Angels ... 51

CHAPTER 10 ... 55
Prepare for Your Encounter ... 55
Preparation is Key to Moving Forward in Life ... 55

CHAPTER 11 ... 59
Working with the Z-Angels ... 59

CHAPTER 12 ... 65
Introducing the Siblings ... 65
Working with these Angels is Paramount for Change ... 65

CHAPTER 13 ... 87
TRILUCE ... 87

CHAPTER 14 ... 91
A Message from God Energy ... 91

CHAPTER 15 ... 95
Living with the Z-Angels ... 95
It is Your Time in Life to have the Most Powerful Connection and Shine in All that You Do ... 95

ACKNOWLEDGEMENTS ... 103
ABOUT THE AUTHOR ... 105

Preface

Z-Angels were drip-fed to me over the last few years. In the beginning, I was shown that four angels would be revealed, and I would share them with the world. At this point, there was no time scale—just a few words from the Universe.

Being a psychic medium for many years, I am used to the 'voices' giving me information about what to expect on my path in the future. The spiritual road I travel is where I make decisions and follow universal guidance.

I have evolved as spiritual energy in a human body, and I have always taken on board everything given to me—mostly learning experiences and not all of which are pleasant. I have noticed that the more evolved I become, the easier the lessons became.

That said, this was one of the most challenging times. I had to write continuously until complete. To bring these angels to you is a movement out of my comfort zone. I have learned to trust and believe that the Universe is giving me all that my soul desires, and with this one, the influx of information was quick, precise, and evolutionary.

I cannot express the excitement as I type this and the rest of the book for you. I see the angels in my mind's eye and all that God's light wants to share with you.

You see, that was another turning point in my life recently, to work with God's given light.

I am told from the God energy to accept the angels of God's light.

This is what I share with you.

Be brave and connect to your heart space as you heal from past trauma. Learn to feel and be ready to receive. Receiving their energy is a blessing from God and will transform your personal and spiritual life.

CHAPTER 1

Introduction

Everything Begins to Make Sense

I was on Earth for 62 years on the 3rd of March 2022.

I am very grateful, proud, and content to have gained so much wisdom and knowledge through my experiences on Earth in my earthly body.

Over ten months ago, I had an epiphany; it was very random and seemed to come out of nowhere.

Do things come out of nowhere, or is there a where that everything comes from?

Such deep emotions swept across me that day. The epiphany struck me with the realisation that I am thrilled with who I am and grateful for the number of years in this earthly body. It was more than that; it was an overwhelming feeling of knowing with a wave of wanderlust in the most serene way. It was a knowing where I was, totally feeling my love, soul, and life. It was the feeling of being exactly where I was supposed to be. It was the most unique, unearthly, yet earthly feeling ever.

Can you imagine that euphoric feeling? Better than most orgasms men have given me! That total tantra experience swept across my mind, body, and soul. I know all that I do is guided by God. On that day, the voice told me that this is how I will live now, in total euphoria, which will stay in this human body throughout my life.

I am grateful.

Angels and me.

Throughout my whole life, I have been working on my spiritual path in various ways, not always realising what it was. Around the age of three, I remember seeing and hearing people and voices that no one else picked up on. There have been many connections to angels in one way or another. I have never felt that deep feeling of being guided by that angelic realm. I have felt driven by something my entire life. I have never learned from books but allowed the Universe to teach me what I needed at a significant time. I am universally taught, and here today, through those teachings to share with you.

Angels are in the Bible, Quran, and other scriptures dating back many years in history, and helpful ways are associated with them.

After being divinely pushed from my teaching career, I have worked as a mystic, author, and psychic medium. I have lived my spiritual path for many years using all my senses and connections beyond what I thought possible, except for angels. It was a car accident that changed my course for the better. A divinely guided smash of two cars led to me being fully embraced by the Universe. I call Archangel Michael to help release and guide others to do the same.

I have experienced many spiritual phenomena and taken part in numerous paranormal sessions. My life has been littered with unaccountable activities in houses, pubs, graveyards, and fields, to name but a few. I believe the Universe guides us and gives us what they know we are capable of, and my work has taken me worldwide.

Voices and words from places where there are no humans make you dig deep to find the answer to who and where the voices are. I can hear voices in the house I live in now; there are footsteps and bangs when I am home alone. People often ask if I am scared because I have seen and heard unaccountable phenomena all my life; it is part of who I am.

There is no logical answer to these happenings except to believe something connects and lets me feel their presence. In many ways, it has been a comfort in my life.

Over the last 40 years, wherever I have lived or stayed, there is always a dark figure with a long-hooded cloak with its head bent down, gliding along the hallway. I have received so much comfort from this. When it comes to the doorway, it usually means I must make a decision or get on with something in my life; it is like a warning. The only time it has gone from the hallway was last week when I saw it in the kitchen. I turned around and bumped into it just before I began writing this! I guess it was bringing forward the urgency to write.

Many people want answers; they want to prove and have proof of the existence of something unearthly. Science helps us keep our minds open as we seek the truth. Science needs spirituality, and spirituality needs science. I will leave it to the scientists to bring the two together, as I know what I know, see, and do.

Time after time, I would look for an answer in human form. Approximately 30 years ago, I realised I was on Earth to do this work and not find the proof. I don't care so much about the proof; the voices, evidence, and confirmation that have come into my life could be nothing other than from non-earthly sources.

I believe.

In a few years, someone will put some electrodes on my head and plug me into a machine, and they will see everything I can. Like watching my spiritual visions live on TV.

That will blow your mind!

I rarely speak of all that comes to me; you would not believe 80% of it. I keep it to myself, knowing it will come out one day. I will be guided at the right time. I am often driven to do work beyond what people know and talk about today. I used to hold back, but this is the beginning of me not holding back. My life's confirmation often comes in a book, a film, or something someone indirectly says. I only have the words in my head. I have no one to tell me that it is okay; I get on and do it.

This is an example of confirmation with this angel work. I listen to an excellent tarot reader on YouTube called Minnow Pond; he is Pisces like me. For the last few months, he has talked about Pisces' ability to think and work beyond what people know; we are here to leave a legacy for others, not necessarily for now. This being way out of my comfort zone is one of those legacies, and thanks to Minnow, I have kept my focus.

I'll try not to go off on a tangent; I am good at that. I want to keep this about the angels, with my background and experiences thrown in.

I have taken time off from writing my novel to put these words to paper. This is a crucial time in my life of change—a critical time for you, too, as there are profound changes to come universally.

Whenever you read this, it is the right time for you.

I am super experienced in channelling and trance work. My channelled words are universal predictions, personal messages, and content that reassures people on Earth that all is well. That evolution is happening and keeping us on track with everything.

There is no holding back. Once something is given to me in trance or channelling, I must type it or record the words. There is this constant need that I must fulfil the task.

Most often, only one word is needed to begin. I used to hold back and wait for a sentence or more in my mind, but now I know better; once I get one word and a feeling of fullness, I begin to type, and the rest flows.

Yesterday evening, I worked on some social media posts I would schedule to save time later. Suddenly, I was told by the voices I hear, not mine or my human thoughts, that God wanted to channel some vital information I needed to share with the world.

Oh, my goodness, I thought—this is it. I am coming out with something out of my comfort zone.

I will always have new things to share with you; I never know when they will drop into my life.

God, eh?

Recently, God has been coming into my work more frequently.

I have always believed in God, and the other day, I had a conversation with my mother about the times I loved going to Sunday school at the local church when I was around five or six years of age. She told me of the weekend when I was ill and was snuggling on the sofa with my favourite blanket. I was asleep and feeling very poorly all Saturday and Sunday morning. My friend called at the house, as we went together to Sunday school, and my mother told her I was too ill to go.

I jumped off the sofa and said I was okay and wanted to go.

I did.

I enjoyed it and went back to the sofa on my return and slept for the rest of the day.

I listen to my body, which tells me what I need to eat, do, and speak.

Being in tune with my mind, body, and spirit is very important in this century.

Occasionally, I have felt unwell before evenings of mediumship and psychic demonstrations.

I always know the Universe will take away what I do not need. They will make me right for the audience. They never let me down. I smile as I type, just as I know that this is right for now.

Over the years, the Universe has shown me what will happen in my life. I never share these predictions with anyone. These are set in stone and cannot be changed. There will be my free will choices intertwining with those specified.

I have always been authentic with my connection to the Universe and worked organically, growing my audience.

I can shout my message loud enough!

Observing others is something I like to do; people watching, they call it.

I am often shown various stages in their lives, where they will go wrong/right and the lies and truths they tell.

I can see everything around everyone that the Universe chooses to show me.

Today, I am sharing the Z-Angels with you to help you grow more efficiently in your life.

We all need a little help.

CHAPTER 2

This is New

Trusting in All I Do

For many years, I have been shown a new wave of angels to be revealed to humans. It has been in my psyche to share them with you. When they told me in dreams, meditations, and visualisations, I had to respond. I briefly shared this with one person, and she tried to make it her own, so I zipped my lips and told no one else! I have seen this coming for years, and now it is here. They drip-feed me.

It is this that I am now sharing with you.

I am beyond excited!

I have a lot of work to do as everything is coming quickly.

I never envisaged how this would happen and often thought it was for another lifetime.

All four have been revealed, and I am simultaneously excited and humbled!

I am very conscious of how new this is and want you to know that they are here as part of Earth's natural evolution.

I remember listening to Wayne Dyer, an American self-help and motivational speaker, on YouTube. He talked about writing a book in a weekend from start to finish. He could not stop writing until it was complete. He felt like a force was giving him everything he needed.

It is very much like that for me; I cannot stop with the Z-Angels: a book, website, social media groups, meditations, and merchandise—all of which have fallen into place quickly.

This is undoubtedly divinely guided and downloaded from God's light energy.

There is this internal confirmation that it is meant to be.

It is incredible to have you as part of the new Z-Angel wave.

Listen to your internal dialogue and bring forward the words which resemble your true soul calling. Listen.

CHAPTER 3

My Preparation

Hindsight is a Wonderful Thing

Do you see the synchronicities in your life? These come in many forms and are often noticed in hindsight. Names, number sequences, letters, places, and many more; think of these as clues. However, if you are super observant of your own life and its events, you will soon become accustomed to seeing synchronicities.

The letter Z and the Z-Angels feel very special to me, and I have not understood why. Archangels Zadkiel and Zaphkiel have given me a feeling in my belly like no other; they could be friends of mine, a love or best friend, or a long-lost relative coming home after years away. That feeling of warmth and contentment. True Love.

It feels right.

I have often asked the Universe why I felt this connection, but nothing returned.

They zipped their lips this time.

Z excites me, Z makes me feel strong and courageous, Z gives me a sense of being, and Z gives me a sense of awesomeness and intense sensations of knowing something is unique. People joked that my next relationship partner would have the initial Z; yet to be revealed.

What is this, I ask?

Maybe a planet will give a vibration that needs translating. A spirit that has passed lets me know they are around and has messages to deliver to others or keeps me on track in my life.

I have previously written books about my spiritual life, downloaded and vibrationally translated sections for the reader. Another Z, my first book—*Zoetic Soul*.

I am thinking about that day, sitting at my computer on the eve of the 4th of January 2022. As I type the date, I wonder if anything happened on that day of significance.

The 2nd of March 2022 was the day before my 62nd birthday! I am searching for that significance, only to realise that the numbers add up to 11:

1+4+2+2+2=11

I have now looked at today's date: 2+3+2+2+2=11

Yesterday, I went to the local grocery store.

The person in front of me spent:	£6.66
I spent:	£14.14
The person behind me spent:	£17.17

I wake up at 4:44, 5:55 etc., wide awake and ready to start working.

Number 11 is a significant number to harness in life. "The start of something new, something divinely guided. Do not miss this opportunity," is what the numerologists say.

Do you see the synchronicities in your life?

There are many more, but I wanted to give you a flavour of those instrumental to this book.

TURKEY, February 2014.

I met an English lady in Turkey who shared stories from the Bible; she read the Bible daily. While drinking that delicious hot, sweet Cay at the tea house in the heat of the midday sun, she invited me on a road trip. Always up for a challenge and new adventure, I agreed to go.

She explained the seven churches in Turkey mentioned in the Book of Revelation.

According to the Book of Revelation, there will be a future ministry of angels. Their work toward God and humanity is not yet finished.

Then I saw another angel flying amid heaven, with the everlasting gospel to proclaim to those who live on the earth—to every nation and tribe and language and people (Revelation 14:6).

Seven Princes of Heaven: Michael, Gabriel, Raphael, Uriel, Sealtiel, Jehudiel, and Barachiel.

Revelation 2.1: To the Angel of the church in Ephesus

Revelation 2.8: To the Angel of the church in Smyrna

Revelation 2.12: To the Angel of the church in Pergamum

Revelation 2.18: To the Angel of the church in Thyatira

Revelation 3.1: To the Angel of the church in Sardis

Revelation 3.7: To the Angel of the church in Philadelphia

Revelation 3.14: To the Angel of the church in Laodicea

Revelation 7.1: 144,000 is mentioned three times in the Book of Revelation—144 is very significant in my life, connecting to my beloved grandmother Mary, who lived to the age of 100 years and six months. She lived her whole life at number 144; she won many raffles with the four numbers and always commented on 4 and 144.

In meditation at the Temple of Apollo, which we visited as it was only a five-minute drive from home, I saw four angels standing at the four corners of the earth, holding back the earth's four winds to prevent any wind from blowing on the land, sea, and trees. This angelic energy was the most divine connection; pale white tipped with mint green.

On another day, we had a beautifully connected meditation during our visit to the temple. I could see the beauty beyond earthly colours and a wonderful, knowing feeling in my mind's eye.

Feel into the meditation visions below.

Lions were padding across the roads in silence and locked their vision into my eyes, transferring thoughts with grace.

Tigers were bringing in strength and visions; the tigers were helping to build strength in people on Earth.

Rainbows were shown to signify unity and oneness, joining oneself and soul as the rainbow colours merged and misted as they faded.

Male faces were shown to me of the old, wise creators and inspirers who had been on the land.

The temple's rebuilding was shown in the future, with restorations and galleons working hard for something they once lost.

Chariots were given as a passage in time, representing the journey. Gold and red with ornate fretted work on the sides of each chariot glistened in the bright light.

In the presence of my soul energy, the meditation gave me so many unearthly moments to bring away with me.

As the meditation ended, I had this overwhelming feeling to plant a seed.

We found what looked like peach stones on the ground and used a loose rock to break the stones to reveal the kernels.

Seeds, as in thoughts, were planted, too, as we meditated and connected to the angelic energies. Each time we meditated, there was a profound connection to angels.

A seed was sown literally and symbolically. And the temple was rebuilt in my meditation.

Early one morning, we drove along the gateway road, the only way in and out of our town. As we turned a corner, a sheep was in the middle of the road. Dead and just lying there.

We both sent healing and helped its soul on its passage to eternity. We said prayers and then had to travel onward. Sheep and lambs are mentioned in the Book of Revelation too.

There were so many signs, warnings, and blessings on this journey. We were picking up confirmations along the way.

At another sacred site, I was spiritually guided to look in the water well situated in the distance diagonally beyond the entrance; sadly, a dead frog was floating, but a living frog accompanied it, yin and yang, right and wrong, left and right.

Everything has a balance; one alive and one dead frog indicated that it was the end of one cycle and the beginning of a new one. I do adore frogs.

We are here to do God's work; how else can it all make sense? Maybe you have a different word for God.

We know our destination, but we have no map. The same can be said for life.

We wandered off to the right on the sacred site littered with rocks on the hard ground, not knowing if it was the right way.

We can see lots of birds.

They are there to guide us.

Birds have been with us many times on our different expeditions, and we believed they guided us and confirmed that all was well for this work.

My psychic, mediumship, and spiritual senses are on fire and ready to guide me; I have been tuned into the site's energies.

As I lean against an ancient dry-stone wall, I can feel myself falling and rising into different dimensions of times gone by. I am in a state of trance now.

I see an army of soldiers in khaki uniforms carrying guns with a sword at the end.

They are driving forward, running as if to start a battle, not running from something.

I then see floodgates opening and water pouring through them.

The water covers a city, which makes us think of Atlantis.

Off on a little tangent: staying in Turkey for a while, friends and family would visit, and we would go to Ephesus, a tremendously sacred site. I distinctly remember one visit and was keen to share with them a particular area where I sat and meditated. We reached the area, and it was all submerged in water. It may have been two years since my previous visit. I asked the local people about this, and they seemed to think it was always this way. I have a picture of it before and after; it is the same place.

We never really know what is submerged, do we?

Back to my visions, they showed me the past to open the gateway to the future.

It is also essential to do this in life to acknowledge the past and let go of it. Letting go enables forward travel.

We have cleansed and opened a gateway for us to work from; we have shone the light to wake and cleanse.

In my mind, I have heard the 12th dimension being spoken for days now, and I remember in a reiki session a few years ago, the Reiki Master Healer Teacher gave me the 12th dimension.

She received a message from God's energy for me. I saw God standing over me while she gave me Reiki; the energy was revealed very slowly, and then I became overwhelmed by the energy. It was the most phenomenal but knowing and safe experience I have ever had;

the energy in my meditation was the same vision as hers. I felt like a child who was receiving precious unconditional love and more.

After the session, she told me I was here to do God's work but not traditionally or religiously. That is it; no explanation or expansion. I have held that in my heart ever since.

This is my opening to that, the 12th dimension.

The Twelfth Dimension

The All That Is; The Source

People say you cannot envision the 12th dimension; I believe I have encountered this many times in meditation and trance work.

In numerology, the number twelve is one and two joined. It represents the fusion of unity (1) and duality (2). Spiritually speaking, it is God. In my opinion, many ancient cultures have defined this God as "beyond words," which it is but not beyond vision.

According to research on the web, whatever we say or think about this dimension, the 12th dimension is never enough. It includes and exceeds all infinities. It is beyond definition and is always more than we can imagine. However, from my experience in a tranced state and intense meditations, I believe it is possible to experience this dimension, and I believe I have.

God is pure, unconditional love. But it is more than that, much more.

Ultimately, this is The Source—all that is and more.

Another sacred day, and we decide to stop for breakfast.

The restaurant is full of chattering people that create a din, but a slightly musical one; Turkish families enjoy their breakfast.

Delicious smells waft around the room as we look for a table outside in the smoking area. I gave up over 25 years ago but tolerate others' habits.

All the smoking tables are in use; we stand a little, then go inside.

The only one free is table number three: the Holy Trinity, the three of God.

So different yet perfectly complementing each other, as a friend has joined us. The three of us today are on this mission together and will gain something individually profound.

We chat and sometimes sit in silence, delicately eating our way through the feast of Kavahalti, a Turkish breakfast consisting of mouth-watering fresh food: eggs, cheeses, sausages, cucumber, tomatoes, honey, cream, various pieces of bread, black and green olives, olive oil, cured meats, fruit preserves, and sweet butter, all served with delicious, heart-warming Cay. It reminded me of the last supper!

Table number three, three people, the Holy Trinity, what more will be revealed?

One of the three thinks they are going through a rebirth, and I wasn't sure, as the Universe told me, a transformation.

I have had my rebirth ready for this trip, not to have the trip for the rebirth; this is what I hear as I type.

Sitting in the back of the car, I contemplate what we might have to encounter next.

We are all silent, getting ready for what is ahead.

I am excited today and know it will be a significant part of our visits; I know the place's name but have done little research. I like to go in cold, so I have no knowledge to influence my thoughts.

I know I will be directly contacted on this trip, from God, from my spirit guides, from Grandmother Mary; she has been with me since she passed over in 2012 at 100 years and six months old, whose birthday is on the 12th of February 1912. No coincidence we are here in her birthday month. You can read about my journey with Grandmother Mary in my other books.

I have an overwhelming sense of angelic energy with me today.

We continue along the bumpy roads, taking in the authentic Turkish landscapes as we pass the sign for Bergama, with only seven kilometres to the centre.

The sign for the site is tucked behind the other signs showing us to turn left up a winding road.

We park up and pay the 15tl to enter. There is Wi-Fi and 3G on Apple, but because of the rain and cloud, it was not working as it should. Or, we're not meant to use it; use your own eyes, someone said in my head.

We look around the Otopark and the few shops open for the winter visitors.

We see a path to follow on our walk to the church/ruins. A local person told us about the paper historically made in the area.

There are information boards, and as we read them, we discover that this site was the first hospital and healing centre.

One sad thing is that pregnant women and those dying are not allowed in; they will not be healed. We can't quite understand that but know they will have had their reasons.

We walk and sense the energy change from warm and uplifting to cold, sad, and emotional. We have experienced many feelings and emotions on this trip, and this place is proving to be no different.

The trees, to me, are impressive, with old limbs and branches so full of history. I had to hug this tree! Was I a tree in another life?

These are occasions where words of the English language are not enough. I felt the wisdom and energy of the tree's years, and then another overwhelming energy embrace as the angel materialised in front of my eyes. I didn't know which angels were with us at each sacred site; it was enough to have them there.

That wonderful thing called hindsight is with me as I type. Thinking that I have had minimal contact with angels in my life, I recall many phenomenal connections, most of which I have seen and felt on sacred sites. As I remember these times, I do feel very blessed. As with most poignant moments, I have been given precisely the perfect connection. It is funny how we don't realise just how special an occasion can be at the time. I am very humbled to have experienced the angels with us on the visit to the sacred sites in Turkey.

Continuing at this site, I went down some steps but then had to climb/jump as the steps ended to get to an area with four pillars at each corner and one in the middle.

My mind's eye is wide open at this site. I was drawn to stand on hard ground with a few white wildflowers around it and place my hand on the broken pillar. I closed my eyes and saw what looked like a bath; I could see people being stripped and washed with cold water. Cleansed. Maybe there was a plague of some sort?

7th February 2014 numerology 7+2+2+1+4=16.   1+6=7

"The Christian doctrine of the Trinity defines God as three divine persons or hypostases: the Father, the Son, and the Holy Spirit; 'one God in three persons.' The three persons are distinct yet are one substance, essence or nature.'" Wikipedia

There are no earthly words; even as I sit today and type, the feelings regurgitate within me. This site gave me so many deep connections to the site's buried history and the energy of God. I was in awe and humbled by the whole visit.

I feel very serene with deep love and such an orgasmic presence, at one with the world.

Close to Ephesus, the Virgin Mary's (Meryemana Evi) house with a shrine and a keyhole-shaped baptismal pool can only be described with incredible eyes and that feeling of walking back in time. If you visit, place yourself on the pathways and stand still for a moment or two to soak up the history, most of which has not been confirmed, but the site has reported visits from various popes.

I packed my bag for two nights away. We would stay with a friend; I knew of her but had not previously met her. She is spiritual.

We stay in another city, ready to travel the following day.

Turkey is not warm this time of year, especially in the old Turkish houses that do not face south. I took my rolled-up quilt, pillow, sheet, and fluffy socks to keep my feet warm.

Like two children going on their first adventure without adults, we were excited to anticipate what we would experience.

Chatting constantly about everything in our lives and what might happen, some of the stuff will be seen as off the wall, mad, or unbelievable. Still, you must remember that we are following our paths repressed over the years by parents, society, family, and the need to survive. Now is our time. We are all at different places in our lives but know we have a connection; we KNOW we are on a journey here in Turkey.

Saturday the 8th of February 2014. Numerology 8+2+2+1+4=17. 1+7=8

I noticed a digital clock on the wall of a building in the car park, seeing it was seconds away from 11:11. We see so many signs in life; do you see those shown to you? In numerology, 11:11 is seen as a gateway, with new openings and new starts.

I believe everything is meant to be in life.

So, 11:11 was perfect timing to begin our road trip today.

Seagulls in abundance swirled towards the car. So many birds were flying in front of the car, and we had to break sharply due to a cat wanting to use one of its nine lives!

And on we go.

I have shared these parts of the journey with you, hoping you allow yourself to have random adventures that present themselves in your life. See all the synchronicities, and find a belief that drives you onward every day.

I believed and had some fantastic visions of the angels at the seven sacred sites in the Revelation journey.

I have a sense of satisfaction, as though I needed to complete the sacred sites before I could move on to more in my life.

A complete circle as I am back working with angels today!

Jan Mayfield

Never underestimate the power of the universe. It will show you the way. Open your eyes.

CHAPTER 4

God's Words

I Have To Do as I am Told

One moment, I am doing some work on the computer, and the next, I have this powerful energy around me.

I dropped what I was doing, compelled to design a graphic depicting angel wings. Everything is so fast: my typing, the images, the colours, the names and where they are from. I cannot stop; the images are there, and words are coming through.

There are four angels.

FOUR ANGELS—WOW!

I have been shown this for years. Now it comes with spectacular colour and speed. The most fragrant, bizarre grand opening is here and delivered to all.

Tada—eureka!

My chest is pounding, my heart is beating, and my breathing is consistent with an athlete sprinting for the finish line. This is very exciting, divinely entrusted to me.

The fat kid with ginger hair who could always do better in school!

Four are significant in previous trance sessions; four earth pillars have been given many times.

Four is strength; in numerology, it is said to be solid and confident, stable, and representative of endurance.

Square in astrology, the number four is related to the north node. This node tells the story of the soul's journey or who you are meant to be in this life.

My north node suggests: "I have an innate awareness of the spiritual dimension of life and am attuned to my nature's higher, lovelier realms. I am using the power of my mind and imagination to keep aligned. I am translating love into service and reconnecting with the feelings of boundless love and compassion within myself. I am compassionate, caring, and forgiving, and I build a foundation to help on a broader scale."

The healing stems from a tremendous power of faith, often shown by miraculous healing in my life and work on higher spiritual dimensions. I could go on, but that about sums up my dedication to helping others and finely tuned to God's energy for this work. I have completed many stages and stay with this one. Reading my north node does feel supremely powerful.

Have you read your north node?

Earth is a circle held up by four corners that speak of the hard work that is the foundational vibration of four. Egyptians believed heaven was supported by four pillars rising out of the earth in ancient times. The Mayan civilisations believed that four beings held the skies aloft.

In the Old Testament in the Bible, four rivers flow into paradise from four corners of the earth. The authors of the New Testament are the four evangelists who spread the message of Christianity after Jesus was nailed to a four-point cross.

Many references to the number four and associations in life bring forward a strength.

The number four, Arba in Hebrew and Arabic, is a cardinal number that frequently occurs in the Old Testament, New Testament, and Holy Quran. It is stability, order, grounded nature, completeness, and comprehensiveness. Allah has determined four to be an adequate number to provide proof beyond doubt or sufficient time.

Four seems to represent the cosmic order and stability of the moon's four phases and the earth's four cardinal points: north, south, east, and west.

I am sharing the fours to connect the four angels and the others in the world's documentation.

Four angels are to be revealed.

I am guided to give you an account of the four angels with God's words. As with all areas of life on Earth, there will be teachings that may not be received as quickly as others. God is here to show you that all instructions are necessary and play an essential role in your life's progression.

Words from God to you:

"I am the light, the love, and purity of the cosmopolitanic world. I am permitting you to be granted the essence of nature and the organic influence of the stars and stratosphere. You will become one with the Z-Angels of my light energy should you wish to travel your etched path of no return. I grant you the wishes and fulfil your soul's desires in life. In my presence, you are love and only love."

I am grateful, thank you.

CHAPTER 5

This is New

Trusting in All I Do

My mind is full, as is my surrounding space. My aura, spiritual mind, and the energies around me are dense on this day. There is no filter or consideration for me as a human. Someone wants to speak through me. They will talk at all costs.

This is it. I remember thinking, this is it.

My belly started to tickle with excitement and anticipation.

I know this is bigger than anything I have shared before.

I have always known this, and now it is going to happen.

The energy then gives me a sense of an ocean wave of love, driving the energy closer and, in a way, giving me a sense of comfort. I know the feeling of love is like no other that I have experienced in this life as a human so far.

Do I want to experience it again? More than anything in the world, I do, so very much.

In my life, when anything has changed spiritually, perhaps a new skill or feeling powerfully connected to the source, it has never been repeated in the same way—always moving forward and getting more significant and profound.

Source—what is the source to you?

God's energy is around me today.

God has been around me since I was a child, but over the last 12 months, I have felt this energy's strength steadily creeping into my life. The intensity and power given in one swoop would have been too overwhelming if released to me in one phase.

The intensity and power have stayed with me. I have this different energy while working and in daily life, akin to having a shift.

The God-energy reveals to me in a vibration what I must translate.

They stopped giving me words long ago and brought the vibration close to me. But this is different, probably comparable to the difference between a tiny starter car and a Lamborghini.

I know this information is to share with people, and the right ones will find it.

The vibration is ready. I am asking questions, but they are ignored.

I can hear the vibration for 'listen' being repeated—listen, listen, listen.

I do as I am told, and the blessed words are with me as I listen.

"I am giving you the names of the four angels who have never been revealed on Earth."

"You are to type this, share it in all ways, and people will benefit from the energy created in words, physical components, and your presence."

"Be prepared for everything around you to change, even how people respond to you."

"This is the start of the time we have told you about for many years."

Here, I pause as I need to take in that information and calm my racing heart, ready to receive more.

This is it.

We are showing you four angels; they are being brought to people on Earth who are ready for the changes. Not everyone will resonate with this energy. It will not be on their radar; they will lose the connection transmitted through me.

I am God's light energy soul source of the Universe, and I send you a new wave of angels for the people.

I can't speak or think, salivating, and my heart pumps my red blood with force. Now is such an exhilarating time to be alive.

CHAPTER 6

Delivery

Here are the Z-Angels

People talk of superpowers and super consciousness for themselves. I felt God transcending supreme love energetically with the vibration to translate.

The names of the God-given angels are here.

While creating the graphics, the first name revealed a letter at a time; well, a word in my head, the spelling of which I was unsure. It came to me one letter at a time.

M   A   N   S   C   U   L   E

Manscule

I remember thinking about its meaning. Googling it, there was nothing, no explanation. If there was a meaning and the word was already used, it would take the authenticity away. That is what I wanted to see: nothing.

This is new.

I take a deep breath and exhale slowly; the next one comes. Akin to having quadruplets, the anticipation is crippling.

Z   I   K   T   O   N

Zıkton (pronounced Zukton)

I go weak at my knees when the z-word pops out quicker than Manscule. You know I resonate with the letter Z. This word has not been documented as an angel or anything else. We are on target with the new angels.

I do trust the Universe. Do you?

One letter at a time reveals the third angel.

Z   A   N   O   L   A

Zanola

This name was more pronounced as it was given letter by letter. This I felt in my base chakra with a sudden grounding deep into the earth's centre. My throat chakra choked my vocal cords and spluttered as I typed, followed by a stream of the uprising energy.

Another Z name, and I feel the strength and power of this angel.

Here we go again, back to the process of one letter at a time.

T   R   I   L   U   C   E

Triluce

Oh, wow—there is a magnificent divine connection creating shivers of anticipation all over my body. My auric field is on fire and reaching out to infinity. There is undoubtedly a divine transcendental force with Triluce. I have an unaccountable feeling of being connected to an energy force with a sacred field of emotional waves, forcing tears to cascade from my eyes. It is so wonderful.

There you have it, four new angels from God's source.

MANSCULE

ZIKTON

ZANOLA

TRILUCE

We are four.

CHAPTER 7

Let's become Acquainted with the Four Angels

TRILUCE The Divine Partner of the three lights (tri) light and luce (light in Latin); the overseer of the three. Codes

The other three lights join with TRILUCE to form the kaleidoscopic patterns.

TRILUCE is a vibrant luminescence with translucent movement around your senses, sight, and visions.

Your imagination will be enhanced as you are connected with the divine partner TRILUCE. The celestial energy reaches the meta pack of stability around GOD.

You will only appreciate this essence when you are enlightened to the sense of *knowing* and not asking and working from that human ego. You will have worked with the other three Z-Angels previously.

ZIKTON The Divine Partner—Vibrations

Divine and bathed in the light of the sunset's orange hue and delicate gold leaf, dazzling is the light of the wings' inner core. The brilliance of the yellow and orange capsular light reflects the essence of ZIKTON.

ZIKTON is bringing one soul, one angel, one connection to you.

When you have fully embraced your soul energy in your human life, you will know that nothing can surpass that feeling—nothing.

Brace yourself for a oneness you have not experienced. You will take off and grow at a speed you have not felt in your life as a human. Only then will ZIKTON connect with you.

Light connects the soul, angel, and you into an extravagance of colour. ZIKTON'S baroque-esque movement towards you will bring immeasurable scales of light and the bracing, divine juice of GOD.

ZANOLA The Divine Partner— Numbers

ZANOLA brings forth the bounding inner power that has lain dormant in humans.

Palladium shades present glimpses of sparse light to form a brightness of power, the divine.

All divine partners of God will only join with you when you are fully connected to the life in the human, which serves your soul without exception.

ZANOLA is the presence of full potential without being overpowering. Religion's greatness and monastic void generate the absolute explosion of power within you.

Bathe in the light to sense the presence as you have the effusion of the divine intervention with ZANOLA.

MANSCULE The Divine Partner—Symbols

Divine pink-tipped with blush rose, as the wings are revealed, they have a gorgeous iridescence of glistening light on the tips of each section—see the magnificence of light around the crown.

The feeling of light energy is a comparable physical wing that might spring to the human mind.

There is nothing human about MANSCULE.

A divine partner of God, this angel, if you allow, will connect you to the emerging angelic wave. Humans will need to do nothing to attract MANSCULE.

There is no gender attached to the wings of MANSCULE or the other angels. The Divine Partner. A mere splash of a human interpretation of wings by the light projected rather than the shape.

MANSCULE will breathe the air of the Universe, detect the patterns of your existence, and grace you with a presence you have never experienced.

You cannot call into your life this energy; you will need to be in the correct balance and evolutionary state of a soul being for the experience to gather around you.

Jan Mayfield

The most precious divine connection is with you today.
Feel It.

CHAPTER 8

Are You Ready?

The Time is Right for You to Meet Your True Self; the Z-Angels are Here to Give You that Opportunity

The Z-Angels will bring you a clue to their existence in the form of:

TRILUCE - CODES — As Triluce vibrationally connects to you, your code's powerful exchange will be given.

ZIKTON - VIBRATIONS — All vibrational energy will realign to that of Z₁kton.

ZANOLA - NUMBERS — The power of numbers forces a solid connection to Zanola. Connect to Jan for your six-digit life number.

MANSCULE - SYMBOLS — You will have a variety of symbols entering your life, and you are likely to be given a unique personal symbol. Jan can download this for you.

These angelic energies are not lightly shared with you. You chose to read this book and, therefore, are ready to receive the essence of the angels.

Please share with others in your circle if you are not in the right place to create changes in your life. There is sure to be one or two who need the angels.

They have a message to pass on to you.

You have a message to pass on to the Universe.

There is no better time than as your eyes skim the pages; there is no better time than right in this moment of connection to forge your relationship.

TRILUCE, ZIKTON, ZANOLA, AND MANSCULE will work

together and enter your heart and energy essence. Please do not call them; allow them to be with you more often.

Through your many experiences, and once you let go of all ego and judgemental behaviour, they will centre around you.

These angels will *not* come to egotistical and judgemental humans.

Together, they provide their semantic God-given light presence with power and trails of love and devotion to the soul's passage through the earth.

Together, there is a sense of unwavering blessings, shadowed by nothing. Trust in them to guide you further in your life in this crucial time on Earth.

If you are carrying baggage from the past, please release this now. Let go of all your restrictions and your emotional connections to the past. We live in the present, the NOW, and this is how the angels will work with you.

Your passion and presence on Earth will be revealed, and you will be able to connect to your soul purpose by allowing the angels to guide you.

Jan Mayfield

You are here on earth; you have a reason and purpose. See it. You will receive directions.

CHAPTER 9

Sensing the Z-Angels

These mighty God-given light-wave angels will come to you on most occasions.

Your connection to the soul and working at the soul level is paramount for God's light-angel connection. Heart-centred blessings with waves of diverse energy patterns may be a little strong at times, and you will wonder what is happening. Trust the process and acknowledge their presence.

In hindsight, as everything is revealed I realised I have known of this in the background my whole life, and sharing it now seems so very special and surreal.

Thank you for being in my life.

You will not have experienced anything like this before, and again, I do not have the earthly words to describe the space as they enter my energy field.

Can you imagine your most divinely connected time in your life and multiply that by tens of thousands or more?

The ultimate God connection brought on waves of cherished strength and purpose.

Listen to your favourite piece of divine music, fall into the sounds and rhythms, and allow your heart and soul to be lifted to a new space.

Embrace the feeling when you exhale with pure knowing, and sigh in their presence.

The four are here for you.

You, as a human, will feel like nothing on Earth because you are working and connecting to these angels. Many previous earthly emotions and times will seem irrelevant, as will material items.

There will be a sense of gliding along every avenue presented to you.

Like nothing you have encountered, internal happiness will be static within you.

People often think they can create happiness through the things they do and who they connect with—family, friends, etc.—but this is not the case. True happiness comes from a static place within you when you release your need for external belongings that seemingly give unsustained happiness.

Connect inwardly, and you will feel the joy of life.

They are here to guide you directly from GOD, divinely. They are not servants but the light source, beaming for you.

Each beam is a form of thought, each ray is a form of healing, and each strobe is a blessing.

The depth and strength of the meanings, messages, and handling are far greater than any existence.

We are in an age where we will see things differently from the reported hierarchy of events that have taken place to date. It is time to get real in the evolution of humans and on Earth.

Connect to the four for your ultimate purpose.

You will sense their power as you release your earthly binds.

CHAPTER 10

Prepare for Your Encounter

Preparation is Key to Moving Forward in Life

Ways to Prepare for your Encounter with the Z-Angels

Triluce, Zıkton, Zanola, and Manscule

Are you serious about making those latent changes and transitions in your life?

Maybe you use manifesting, but nothing happens with your manifestations. They may be weak or not what you were expecting, totally misaligned.

You may feel that the Universe is not guiding you where you think you should be.

You know your soul is here for more, and you cannot see it for yourself.

It takes a strong presence, perseverance, and commitment to be so deeply connected that you live your life most divinely.

God's wave of light Z-Angels will caress you into the being you came here to be.

In the beginning, you will need to work on yourself, letting go of the past, believing and living in the NOW, and presenting yourself to the Universe in that non-judgemental, egoless way.

You don't have too much to do at this point in your life. Like other things in life, the last rows in knitting or the last few streets in a driving test can seem endless and often cause more problems. This is when many people give up.

We *want* to take you past giving up.

We *will* take you past giving up.

Are you ready?

I am in love with myself, my inner core, and my soul.

We will connect to the Universe and give you ideas on how to be ready for the Z-Angels to bring their energies to you and help you solidify all that is not for all that is to be.

To live in your intended way will create waves of passion. Be ready.

CHAPTER 11

Working with the Z-Angels

It is essential in life to be guided and allow guidance.

I have allowed guidance all my life but have not always noticed it in the moment. I do now, and I live by the Universe's direction.

Needing to be in a suitable space is critical here. This is not without hard work on your part. Working with the Z-Angels is a choice; if you choose to do so, you will encounter unprecedented changes in your life.

You can do many exercises to release what does not serve you.

You might like to say a mantra repeatedly until you feel a shift.

1 — Here is an example of a mantra written for you:

Thank you, Z-Angels, for our encounter.

I am ready to release all that does not serve me.

I am ready to be released from my emotional ties to the past.

I am ready to accept that I live in the NOW.

Please release me now. Thank you.

Z-Angels, please bring your energies around me once the release is complete.

Thank you. I am grateful.

2 — Writing down what you hold on to is another good way to release yourself from your past. This can be something spoken to you that keeps playing in your mind or an action/event from someone previously that still haunts you.

Take a piece of A4 paper.

Make sure you do this for one person or one action at a time.

Take a deep inhale and exhale slowly through your mouth.

Put your pen on the paper and write anything that comes to your pen.

Fill the page with words, sentences, and pictures. Whatever you feel like putting on the paper, please do it.

Rip the paper up into tiny pieces.

Burn the paper in a safe place.

Now, flush the ashes down the toilet!

Write it. Rip it. Burn it. Flush it.

The words and feelings are gone into the ocean. You will still have the memory, but you cannot feel the emotions; therefore, no connection can hold you back when the emotions are taken away.

This can be performed numerous times and may need to be done more than once for each event.

3 — Accept that everything happens for a reason; accept that you cannot change someone else's actions. I would do this with a mantra:

Never be the reaction to someone's action.

Here is a mantra specifically for you:

I accept all past actions in my life from other people.

I am ready to release my emotional connection to them.

Please release me now.

I release everything as it is stored in my subconscious mind.

I am ready now to see the light of the Z-Angels and be fully immersed in their unconditional love.

Please release me now.

Thank you, fill me with the abundance I need, please.

4 — I am adding number four as I think it is essential to look at the language you use in your life. If you use negative words, you will need to change these to positive ones. Practice this, and you will soon notice a difference.

The power of the word

"As long as a word remains unspoken, you are its master; once you utter it, you are its slave." IBN GABIROL (SOLOMON BEN JUDAH) (c1021 – c 1204), SPAIN

If you say you are struggling in life, you might want to change it to:

My life is abundant; show me the changes.

The significance of this little change can be dramatic.

Take time to write down the negative words you use and what you can change them to.

Now, make a concerted effort to change.

Doing this will create a new energy vibration, and changes will come to you. In the future, take stock of the negative words you speak and think; you will see you have reduced them significantly.

By working on the four ways of releasing, you will notice a difference in your life. You will see changes around you and within.

People on your path will seem different and move on in their lives and often out of yours. They have no significance in your life now.

With a new outlook and feeling different, you will understand that small releases have an overall effect and contribute to the bigger picture. This is a taste of more significant changes.

Other people may come up to you and say you look different; you will to them as your light shines more brightly. They might be unable to put their finger on why you look different. This is an inner glow of knowing.

Now, you are nearly ready to work with the Z-Angels—or, should I say, for the Z-Angels to work with you.

Jan Mayfield

The presence of the Angels will guide you daily. Allow it.

CHAPTER 12

Introducing the Siblings

Working with these Angels is Paramount for Change

Z-Angels of God's given Light

Bringing permission to enter the gateway of the divine

GOD'S LIGHT

TRILUCE

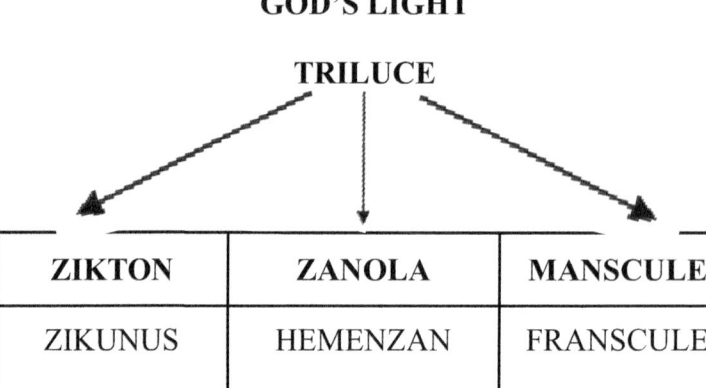

ZIKTON	ZANOLA	MANSCULE
ZIKUNUS	HEMENZAN	FRANSCULE
ZIKBIR	DOOZAN	ZANSCULE
ZIKTEN	SHIMDIZAN	ZAPSCULE
ZIKNUMEN	NIGHZAN	DAIZSCULE

Allow me to introduce you to the siblings of Zikton, Zanola, and Manscule. They are here to prepare your space and vibration, giving you the release you need to connect to Zikton, Zanola, and Manscule.

Triluce is an overseer of the three; only when your vibration and frequency permit will you connect to the energy of Triluce.

Each of the Z-Angels' siblings works on their own vibrational numbers. You can receive your number and message by connecting with Jan in the groups for the Z-Angels or by taking a look at her website for more information: Z-angels.com.

On the following pages, you will read about each Z-Angel and their siblings and their specific way of helping you; follow this, and you will soon see a difference in your life.

I have found that some dedication is required; this does not happen overnight, and you must be prepared to consistently commit to working with the Z-Angels and their siblings.

Find a rhythm in your life as you adjust to this work, as this work will reward you in ways you cannot imagine.

ZIKTON

ZIKTON (Pronounced Zukton) and the siblings shown here are the Z-Angel energy that will bring you to a place of connected power after you have released all that is not for you from your subconscious mind.

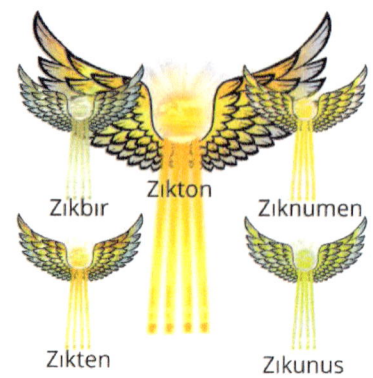

You cannot ask for ZIKTON, as this vibration will get to you when you are super released and prepared.

You may ask the siblings to come to you and help prepare for ZIKTON, and then ZIKTON will work with you to prepare you for your ultimate TRILUCE connection.

Let's begin to connect to the siblings.

Take a deep inhale, right into your belly. Hold it for a moment, then release it slowly through your mouth. Do this three more times.

The siblings of ZIKTON work with vibration and frequency; you will attract the right one to work with you.

ZIKTON — Zıkunus, Zıkbir, Zıkten, Zıknumen

Each has their own vibrational number

| **Zıkunus** | 8846 | **Womb Releasing** |
| **Zıkbir** | 8558 | **Birth–3 Releasing** |

Zıkten	8396	Age 3–5 Releasing
Zıknumen	8972	Age 5–7 Releasing

Close your eyes and think of yellow, orange, gold, and all other forms of the colours; think sunset and sunrise. You will see the colour in your mind's eye if you can visualise it. If not, ask for the colour to be with you; you may want to hold something yellow or gold.

Breathe deeply and release slowly as you ask the siblings to come around you. Take your time with this work, and the benefits will shine brightly on your soul's path.

The power of these numbers gives you the strength to ascertain your soul's intentions. Soon, you will notice changes in your body, mind, and spirit; this powerful vibrational frequency will begin to negate the negativity in your life and bring forth the presence of your passions and soul's lust for life.

Let's connect to the siblings and their mantras.

Zıkunus 8846 Womb Releasing

Womb releasing — In the womb, you will hear and feel many environmental events. Many words are spoken, and endless scenarios exist during that nine months in the womb. You could listen to your parents arguing, speaking positively, talking about someone dying, talking about not being able to afford a baby, and so much more.

As you connect to your soul energy in later life, you must release all emotional ties to the subconscious's memory of your time in the womb. This will eliminate pressure and buried links that may stop you in life. Call Zıkunus to help you.

Releasing from the womb mantra, repeat as many times as you need to.

Thank you, Universe/God, for everything I experienced in my mother's womb.

I am now ready to release all that does not serve me.

I am ready to release all my emotional connections to this time.

Show me, thank you.

I am ready to fill my life with abundance, and I am ready to thrive in my intended way.

Show me, thank you.

To **connect** you and **Zıkunus** — In your mind or spoken aloud, repeat the following mantra as many times as possible, with one hand on your heart centre and one on your solar plexus.

"I connect to the powerful energy force of **Zıkunus (pronounced Zukunus)** — *8846. I am ready to receive all that will bring me to a place of being; I allow guidance* — *8846, 8846, 8846, 8846, 8846, 8846, 8846, 8846. Thank you."*

The power of this sibling and you are now connected.

Zıkbir 8558 Birth–3 Releasing

As with the womb releasing with Zıkunus, Zıkbir is here to cast your subconscious from all emotional ties to the time of birth to three years old.

Do this as soon as possible to release yourself from your past. As an adult, you are unlikely to remember all life events at that age and things that were incorrect. It is a good idea to release all. Ask Zıkbir to release you, enabling you to connect closer to your soul energy vibration of now.

Releasing from birth to three years old mantra, repeat as many times as you need to.

Thank you, Universe/God, for everything I experienced from birth to three years old.

I am now ready to release all that does not serve me.

I am ready to release all my emotional connections to this time.

Show me, thank you.

I am ready to fill my life with abundance, and I am ready to thrive in my intended way.

Show me, thank you.

To **connect** you and **Zıkbir** — In your mind or spoken aloud, repeat the following mantra as many times as possible, with one hand on your heart centre and one on your solar plexus.

"I connect to the powerful vibrational frequency of **Zıkbir– (Pronounced Zukbir)** *— 8558. I am ready to receive all that will bring me to a place of being; I allow guidance — 8558, 8558, 8558, 8558, 8558, 8558, 8558, 8558. Thank you."*

The power of this sibling and you are now connected.

Zıkten 8396 Age 3–5 Releasing

With school and nursery taking up most of your day, learning to speak, hearing others, and tasting new food and drink, a lot is going on.

Not being with your parents is a significant upheaval for many. You will have stored the sad times connecting to this and other events. With Zıkten, concentrate on the ages three to five; these ages are notoriously tricky and easy to keep emotional ties.

Find time in your day to connect and ask Zıkten to release ages three, four, and five for you.

Releasing from three to five years old mantra, repeat as many times as you need to.

Thank you, Universe/God, for everything I experienced from three to five years old.

I am now ready to release all that does not serve me.

I am ready to release all my emotional connections to this time.

Show me, thank you.

I am ready to fill my life with abundance, and I am ready to thrive in my intended way.

Show me, thank you.

To **connect** you and **Zıkten** — In your mind or spoken aloud, repeat the following mantra as many times as possible, with one hand on your heart centre and one on your solar plexus.

"I connect to the powerful vibrational energy force of **Zıkten (Pronounced Zukten)** — *8396. I am ready to receive all that will bring me to a place of being; I allow guidance — 8396, 8396, 8396, 8396, 8396, 8396, 8396, 8396. Thank you."*

The power of this sibling and you are now connected.

Zıknumen 8972 Age 5–7 Releasing

There is a big, wide world out there, and you understand more about it; your vocabulary is growing, as is your knowledge. You believe everything you are told as you know no difference. Another sister or brother may be born in your family; someone may have passed over.

You look up to your elders and are guided by them: teachers and anyone else who is seen to be teaching you. They are not always right, and you learn this as you get older; by that time, it is too late. You have all the emotions stored, affecting your life now. Your soul is here for a different reason, and yours needs to grow in the century you live in, not in generations past.

Be kind, gently ignore their way, and connect to the power of your inner guide, your soul, for clarity and clearance on your pathway to passion.

Releasing from five to seven years old mantra

Thank you, Universe/God, for everything I experienced from five to seven years old.

I am now ready to release all that does not serve me.

I am ready to release all my emotional connections to this time.

Show me, thank you.

I am ready to fill my life with abundance, and I am ready to thrive in my intended way.

Show me, thank you.

To **connect** you and *Zıknumen* — In your mind or spoken aloud, repeat the following mantra as many times as possible, with one hand on your heart centre and one on your solar plexus.

"I connect to the powerful vibrational energy force of ***Zıknumen (Pronounced Zuknumen)*** *— 8972. I am ready to receive all that will bring me to a place of being; I allow guidance — 8972, 8972, 8972, 8972, 8972, 8972, thank you."*

The power of this sibling and you are now connected.

You can alter the mantra for individual years if you find yourself still a little stuck. For example, if you know of a bad experience at the age of six, include age six only.

The mantra changes how you hold onto the past by releasing your emotional connection, leaving you with the memory and no feelings.

You can gauge this by thinking of an event or age and noticing what feelings arise inside you. If there are none, then it is complete. Think of this as a process, not a quick fix.

ZANOLA

ZANOLA and the siblings shown here are the Z-Angel energy that will bring you to a place of inner power, creation, and connection to your soul. Work with ZANOLA'S siblings to find that space deep within you on which you will thrive.

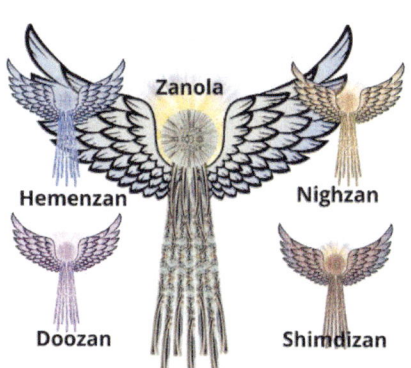

You cannot ask for ZANOLA to come to you. This vibration will find its way to you.

You may ask the offspring to come to you and help prepare for ZANOLA, and then ZANOLA will work with you to prepare you for your TRILUCE connection.

Let's begin to connect to the siblings.

ZANOLA — Hemenzan, Doozan, Shimdizan, Nighzan

Each has their own vibrational number

Hemenzan	4972	**Speak from your heart**
Doozan	4486	**Speak from your connection to the earth**
Shimdizan	4783	**Déjà vu**
Nighzan	4369	**Vortex fields**

Close your eyes and think of lilac, pale blue, peach, and pale pink; think palatial with platinum and palladium and all shades in between.

You will see the colour in your mind's eye if you can visualise it. If not, ask for the colour to be with you; you may want to hold something white-gold or platinum or a pale blue piece of fabric.

Breathe deeply and release slowly as you ask the siblings to come around you. Take your time with this work, and the benefits will shine brightly on your soul's path.

Continue with the other siblings.

The power of these numbers and repeating the mantra brings forth the bounding inner strength, which often lays dormant in you.

You will begin to feel awake!

Soon, you will notice changes in your body, mind, and spirit; this powerful vibrational frequency will begin to negate the negativity in your life and bring forth the bounding inner power and soul's lust for life.

Zanola will bring the internal powerhouse often dormant and resisted by humans who ignore their soul's wants and needs. Zanola will refresh your soul connection and open you up to your passion and purpose in this life.

Let's connect to the siblings.

Hemenzan 4972 Speak from your heart

You are connecting to the energies of Hemenzan and asking to be given clarity on your heart centre. Connect to the vortexes of plenty within to share your soul's chosen words in your life.

Sit with Hemenzan and allow your heart vortex to open fully. You must release all past traumas connecting to the heart to do this; for example, *accepting the love lost in the past and forgiving as much as you can from past lovers in your life.*

Release that connection to fathers and mothers who have wronged you on your path, which you still carry in your heart vortex.

Your voice will soon sound different in quality, clarity, and vibration; the deeper you connect to Hemenzan, the louder your voice will become. Find that inner strength, and you will begin to speak the words fluently using the correct connotations, and people will sit up and listen to you.

To **connect** you and *Hemenzan* — In your mind or spoken aloud, repeat the following mantra as many times as possible, with both hands on your heart centre.

"I connect to the soul energy and join with **Hemenzan** *— 4972. I am ready to recognise all that is within my inner being. I am ready; guide me — 4972, 4972, 4972, 4972. Thank you."*

Doozan 4486 Speak from your connection to the earth

As you connect to the energy of Doozan, you will be shown a deep understanding of why you are here. The depth of the connection goes deep into the earth.

Visualise all the rocks and crystals deeply seated in the middle of the earth. Ask for yourself to be grounded and connected to the stability you will feel from Doozan.

Imagine the roots of the oldest oak tree growing out of your feet, winding their way into the earth.

This will manifest a sense of true worth and divine connection. The world will envelop your whole self to give you that static place from which you can pivot.

Ask Doozan to bring this to you using prayer, mantra, or meditation.

You will know you have succeeded with this connection when you do not feel emotionally obliged and reach out in too many directions at any time.

To **connect** you and *Doozan* — In your mind or spoken aloud, repeat the following mantra as many times as possible, with both hands on your heart centre.

"I connect to the soul energy and join with **Doozan** *— 4486. I am ready to recognise all that is within my inner being. I am ready; guide me — 4486, 4486, 4486, 4486. Thank you."*

Shimdizan 4783 Déjà vu

When you feel out of sorts, like there is nowhere to go and no one to see, you feel a little confused as though there is something to do, but you are unsure what it is. There is a strange feeling in your belly that something is about to happen, but you don't know what. Ask Shimdizan to call and see you. *Place your hands on your belly as you ask to be given or shown how to help yourself.*

Close your eyes and allow the connection to be.

Join Shimdizan to receive clarifications in your life. All you need will be given.

Monitor the times you feel you have been here before, knowing that you have visited a place but are unsure when.

Write these times in your notebook.

Think of it as erasing them from your subconscious mind as you note them. Allow this to happen.

You will recognise your success in this connection when you feel the flow of energy and movement in the path of your life and knowing you are ready to take action.

To **connect** you and ***Shimdizan*** — In your mind or spoken aloud, repeat the following mantra as many times as possible, with both hands on your heart centre.

"I connect to the soul energy and join with **Shimdizan** *— 4783. I am ready to recognise all that is within my inner being. I am ready; guide me — 4783, 4783, 4783, 4783. Thank you."*

Nighzan 4369 Vortex fields

Nighzan is filled with helium energy to help you travel to the universal vortex fields. You will travel high into the atmospherics and feel connected to something you know but don't know. Within the areas, you will access many forms of healing.

Nighzan is taking you to places beyond where you have never been before. Do not be surprised if you suddenly like or are attracted to different things after this encounter. You are ready to receive healing of the universal kind. The healing God-given through Nighzan will set you on a path of discovery.

Your connection to Nighzan will balance your body, mind, and spirit. You will likely revisit this healing because it feels like nothing on Earth. You will have a sense of wholeness too.

To **connect** you and *Nighzan* — In your mind or spoken aloud, repeat the following mantra as many times as possible, with both hands on your heart centre.

"I connect to the soul energy and join with **Nighzan** *— 4369. I am ready to recognise all that is within my inner being. I am ready; guide me — 4369, 4369, 4369, 4369. Thank you."*

MANSCULE

MANSCULE and the siblings shown here are the Z-Angel energy that will bring you to the merging angelic frequency patterns. Work with MANSCULE'S siblings to find that internally located and divinely driven pattern of existence.

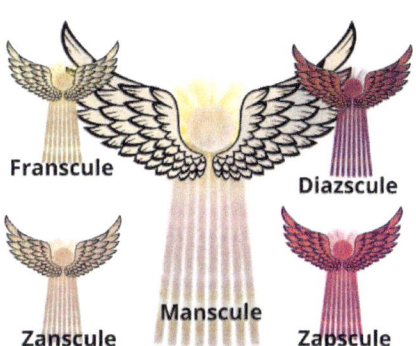

You cannot ask for MANSCULE to come to you. This vibration will find its way to you.

You may ask the siblings to come to you and help prepare for MANSCULE; MANSCULE will work with you to prepare you for your TRILUCE connection.

Let's begin to connect to the siblings.

MANSCULE — Franscule, Zanscule, Zapscule, Daizscule

Each has their own vibrational number

Franscule — 2612 **Belief**

Zanscule — 2432 **Trust**

Zapscule — 2153 **Faith**

Daizscule — 2522 **Grace**

Close your eyes and think of pink, splatterings of blush rose, and luminescence of glistening light. You will see the colour in your mind's eye if you can visualise it. If not, ask for the colour to be with you; you may want to hold something pink—a piece of fabric will suffice.

Breathe deeply and release slowly as you ask the siblings to come around you. Take your time with this work, and the benefits will shine brightly on your soul's path.

The power of these numbers produces the vibration for you to connect to the merging angelic frequency. Soon, you will notice shifts in your emotional needs and wants; this powerful vibrational frequency will balance and refresh your energy fields and external vortex collaboration.

Let's connect to the siblings.

FRANSCULE 2612 Belief

Franscule's energy will give you many experiences to help your belief in life.

What do you believe in, and what do you need to focus on?

Think about that question when you are guided to face your belief. A belief is not a religion as such; it is something you can focus on that will bring strength to you. It will enable you to have power in all areas of your life. It is that of the soul energy that needs daily focus.

The longer you sit with Franscule, the more balanced you will begin to feel. That power within your soul needs to see the focus on your own belief.

You may be thinking, what belief can I have? I do not believe in anything.

You can believe in angels, God, planets, moons, stars, aliens, sausages, and your soul; these are but a few things you can focus on with a belief.

Your focus will allow Franscule to bring all you need, but first, you are asked to show that you can find your belief. This is not static and is very likely to change over time; the point is that you show you can do this now.

Hold your arms up high with your palms to the sky.

In your mind or spoken aloud, repeat the following mantra as many times as possible:

"I connect to the soul energy and join with **Franscule** *— 2612. I am ready to recognise all that is within my inner being. I am ready; guide me — 2612, 2612. Thank you."*

ZANSCULE 2432 Trust

Zanscule is observing you and looking for the things you place your trust in. We often see people trusting in the wrong areas of their lives; 99% of people will do this when they are not flowing in their lives.

Take a little time and think about what you trust and why you do not have trust. Maybe something happened in your past, and now you trust nothing and no one. Well, this will not get you anywhere; it is time to stop using the past as a reason not to trust. Use this as a time to trust for your future self.

Trust what?

Find something to trust; I tend to trust all things non-earthly. The Universe is what I trust, and the Z-Angels and God and everything non-earthly. Over time, my trust has changed and grown into something my 11-year-old self would not recognise. Trusting is to show Zanscule you are serious about making changes and living your most passionate soul self.

Hold your arms up high with your palms to the sky.

In your mind or spoken aloud, repeat the following mantra as many times as possible:

"I connect to the angelic emergence and join with **Zanscule** *— 2432. I am ready to recognise all that is within my inner being. I am ready; guide me — 2432, 2432. Thank you."*

ZAPSCULE 2153 Faith

Many people wonder how they can have faith in life when so many bad things have destroyed much of what they had faith in.

Isn't faith the same as a belief?

Not at all; think of having faith and a knowing in something you believe in. Here, we are talking about faith in you. You are reading this as you know something has slipped, and you need to regain your confidence in your inner self and inner soul energy to bring yourself to the **perfection you were born to ascend to.**

All the work you will do with the Z-Angels is about connecting to the inner you, which is the essence of why you are here on Earth. Have faith that your inner soul resides in your human body and will help you transcend. Speak of this faith as you connect to Zapscule.

Hold your arms up high with your palms to the sky.

In your mind or spoken aloud, repeat the following mantra as many times as possible:

"I connect to the angelic emergence and join with **Zapscule** *— 2153. I am ready to recognise all that is within my inner being. I am ready; guide me — 2153, 2153. Thank you."*

DAIZSCULE 2522 Grace

Maybe you like to think of grace as letting go of a past wrong done to you. You are releasing a wrong done to you and the person who did this wrong away from your mind, body, and soul. With grace, you release and regenerate your life.

It is crucial to balance not needing material things and people who create a feeling of suffocation and pressure in your life. Eliminate these, and you will find a place of beauty, a sanctuary within, and a heart beating to your newfound self's rhythm.

Think of grace as a freedom movement between your past accountability and your present peace of mind. You can connect to grace by surrendering, forgiving, connecting to your faith and trust, being thankful for everything in your life, and being ready to receive blessings.

Hold your arms up high with your palms to the sky.

In your mind or spoken aloud, repeat the following mantra as many times as possible:

"I connect to the angelic emergence and join with **Daizscule** *— 2522. I am ready to recognise all that is within my inner being. I am ready; guide me — 2522, 2522. Thank you."*

CHAPTER 13

TRILUCE

TRILUCE

This is a phenomenal Z-Angel, with a direct connection to the beaming light of God.

You will undoubtedly be led to a wondrous place with many visions beyond what you have ever seen—feelings you have never felt and a connection beyond what you thought possible. You will be given a new channel to work in, bringing forward all that is needed for your soul in this incarnation.

As I type this, my mouth is salivating, and I feel a sense of urgency in my solar plexus.

My heart centre is beating to the energy of Triluce. All the Z-Angels bring their worth and will assist you in connecting to all that you need to, to release from what holds you back. I find it gratifying and humbling to link to this work and Triluce.

It is to create that space where you can flow eternally at this time in your life. The reason you came to Earth will be slowly revealed to you by letting go of the past, past lives, and ancestral lineage. You have the tools for this in the previous chapters.

You came here as a pure soul, and this is your intended pathway. Your connection to your soul, your inner core, is the most precious thing in your time on Earth.

Please step aside from your human you and connect to your inner soul space.

Triluce will work with you once you have introduced yourself to the other Z-Angels and their siblings. Each has four siblings, and there are three Z-Angels before you connect to Triluce. Connect to each of the siblings, then the Z-Angel of that family. It is best not to skip any of the siblings, as this will result in you having to go back and reconnect later, or it will stop you from moving on as you should.

Everyone on Earth will have the opportunity to connect fully to their soul's purpose in life. You will all choose the time right for you. The time you *think* is right might not be what your soul requires. Think about this.

Get out of your way to make way for your soul connection.

Make today your day of commitment.

No matter what you have in your life, there are blessings from God's light energy source and the connection to the Z-Angels.

Do not waste a moment.

Stop procrastinating.

A personal message from Triluce for you today.

There are many people on Earth and there is only one you. You are the reason to jump into the stream of life and allow yourself to grab the handles of life on Earth. It is you and only you who will be the success or failure.

If you choose failure, you will always be wondering what could have been.

If choose success everyday will have an elation of success in varying degrees. You and only you can see the successes in everything you do. The times when you might be down or have earthly elements to deal with will still have an element of success. Find it!

Flow in life is simply that, a flow from one place to another.

We, God, and I, Triluce are the only source connection you need, this connection will bring you faith and abundance. Take the blessings and grow.

Believe we can guide you, ask and you shall be given.

Praise the sun, moon, and stars every day for your blessings.

Remember by name Triluce, the three of light. Blessed by God energy always.

Receive.

CHAPTER 14

A Message from God Energy

A MESSAGE FROM GOD

I am channelling words from God, and there is an overwhelming sense of people needing to hear this.

"I bring for you my light source energy as given to TRILUCE, who is the only one entrusted to do this work with the souls on Earth.

"You will know your Soul requires something more than is currently around you. You will see the need to make corrections on Earth.

"The people of the lands far away from their intended place will have a consequence. This will be given to them via a different vortex, and you should not concern yourself with the details.

"On Earth, in your human body, you should be bonding with your soul on all levels, working with the Z-Angels, and growing the love and peace intended on Earth.

"I do not mean there will be no experiences other than peace.

"It is a mirage you see that creates the problems; then you allow your human self to make them yours. They are not and were never intended to be.

"I have to take action, and today is the day.

"Action from my light source energy as I bring to Earth the transversal powers to grow life to its intended place. To eliminate those who travel far beyond their space and create an ambience of disorder for others.

"It is this disorder that will bring about the splitting of the earth. Those who now work with the Z-Angels and their soul will move to the concord of harmony and joy to the highest frequency vortex.

"In the vortex of holographic space and time, you will harmonise with all living things and implement grace and joy in life and soul energy on Earth.

"I am the one who greets you in all your majestic times and sends you the vibration from which to work. Only when you ignore this will you become ill and wonder about life. Life is about peace, joy, and harmony.

"Thank you to Jan, who has unfaltering energy with her connection and vibrational translations to enable me to speak my truth to you. She will leave many legacies for all in earthly years to come.

"Advice to a truth-seeker: 'Rather than continuing to seek the truth, simply let go of your views.' BUDDHA (C563 – C483BC) India."

To become precious in mind, body, and soul is to become at one with the one.

Soul is precious, as is your connection; feel its presence and glow with joy and pride. Shine your light.

CHAPTER 15

Living with the Z-Angels

It is Your Time in Life to have the Most Powerful Connection and Shine in All that You Do

Moving on

We all know that, after learning something new, it is easy to lose momentum and begin to turn back to old ways. You must release old habits. They are NOT your comfort blanket.

Please do not allow yourself to revert; instead, permit the Z-Angels to help you as they know what your soul requires.

Find peace with your soul, and with that presence, you will find an addiction to feeling good!

Continually release from the past with the exercises. Like the onion layers, each layer reveals another layer; let go of all and emerge to your inner being.

Make it a matter of course; as soon as you sense a slight change in your vibrational energies, connect to the angel who is here with their expertise.

Sometimes it is enough to gaze at the angels, and you will be drawn to the one who will help you today. That is your inner knowing in sync with your needs.

Use the Z-Angel mystic cards; this is a set of 22 cards infused with the Z-Angel energies that Jan has created to enhance your experience with the Z-Angels. Take off the top card; this is the angel you need today. Shuffle and hold the deck to your heart centre for a few moments.

Chant the numbers of the siblings to bring your energy and theirs together. Only when you have worked with all the siblings, Zanola,

Zikton, and Manscule will you have that connection to TRILUCE.

Your path is YOUR everything you need to fall into place at the right time.

Create new routines in your life, and you will soon see the old ones disappear. Create a space for you, your time to work with the angels. By creating this daily, it will become part of your life. Paramount is the connection, love and devotion to the Z-Angels.

TRUST in the power.

I see YOUR light.

Angels at a glance		
Chapter 11 is your key to all Z-Angel connections and how to prepare for working with the siblings		
Triluce Z-Angel Codes	Only after you have worked with the other angels and released.	The most powerful of the Z-Angels.
Zikton Z-Angel Vibrations	Connect to the siblings then Zikton will be ready for you.	A powerful soul oneness connection.
Zanola Z-Angel Numbers	Connect to the siblings, and then Zanola will be ready for you.	Release your inner power.
Manscule Z-Angel Symbols	Connect to the siblings then Manscule will be ready for you.	Connect to the force emerging angelic wave.

Zıkton and siblings		A powerful soul oneness connection.	Connect to the siblings of Zıkton to release your womb to seven links.
Zıkunus 8846		Travels within.	Womb releasing.
Zıkbir 8558		Release trauma.	Birth–3 years releasing.
Zıkten 8396		I will show you.	3–5 years releasing.
Zıknumen 8972		Be creative today.	5–7 years releasing.
Zanola and siblings		Release your inner power.	Connect with the siblings of Zanola to find your internal space to thrive from.

Hemenzan		Speak from your heart.	Release all past trauma within your heart.
Doozan 4486		Speak from your connection to the earth.	Manifest your true worth.
Shimdizan 4783		Déjà vu.	Receive clarifications in your life.
Nighzan 4369		Vortex fields.	Balance in mind, body, and spirit, taking you beyond what you know.
Manscule and siblings		Connect to the force of the emerging angelic wave.	Manscule will find you.
Franscule 2612		Belief.	Find your belief, and Franscule will be in focus.
Zanscule 2432		Trust.	Show your trust to reveal your passionate soul self.

Zapscule 2153		Faith.	To reveal the perfection you were born to ascend to.
Daizscule 2522		Grace.	Freedom of movement between past and present, peace of mind.

Z-Angels

With love

xx

Jan Mayfield

ACKNOWLEDGEMENTS

In the main, I acknowledge my constant teachings from the Universe, Angels, Z-Angels, and God and all my trance and channelling work to date.

I thank all those who have been instrumental on my path and those who have shown a dislike for me and my work, as this has given me the impetus to carry on.

Minnow Pond, you and your tarot readings on YouTube have shown me the real Pisces and my ability to forge ahead with my work. A fellow Piscean who speaks the same language.

I am eternally grateful to my dear friend and our adventures in Turkey, and I feel blessed to know you.

To all my other connections worldwide, I thank you for your blessings and bonds, never to be broken.

To all of you reading this, shake up your life and LIVE!

Jan Mayfield

ABOUT THE AUTHOR

The eternal universal scholar with a thirst for life and all things non-earthly, Jan has grown beyond recognition over the last three decades with her endeavours to help those who seek their true purpose, passion, and rightful place on Earth.

Rising from an illness, she began to release her true self using a sequence of coordinated events.

She shifted from teaching in adult education to teaching in various forms in the spiritual sense.

Her passion is to share the words of the Universe, God, and Z-Angels, knowing they will find the right ears.

Jan sees life through a very different set of glasses. She is never stuck on ideas of intuitively helping others. Her unique vision, trance, channelling, and approach bring insight and empowerment to her clients.

She is a dedicated soul on a mission who unconditionally aids you in your life.

www.z-angels.com

www.janmayfield.com

All social media updates will be given on Jan's websites

TT Janmysticangels

YT Jan Mayfield

BOOKS

Zoetic Soul – pertaining to life, your life

Inspirational Women of the World – co-author

Journaling for 30 days

Z-Angels Notebook

Z-Angels — A gentle but powerful nudge in life comes at the most opportune moment.

This is yours.

Z-Angels mystic oracle cards, 22 cards infused with the Z-Angels' energy vibration.

Jan Mayfield

Printed in Great Britain
by Amazon

85824429R10068